PICTURE BOOK
OF
SCOTLAND
IN COLOUR

PICTURE BOOK
OF
SCOTLAND
IN COLOUR

Colin Bell

PEERAGE BOOKS

Half title: The floodlit ramparts of Edinburgh Castle are as impressive a sight as any in the capital, stirring the emotions of Scots and tourists alike. A castle has stood on this site for more than 1,000 years and signs of Iron Age habitation have been found on the rock.

Title page: Picturesque Loch Achray nestles in the heart of the Trossachs just north of Aberfoyle. Nearby the 1750-feet summit of Ben A'an affords splendid views of the entire area.

Right: A chilling wintry dawn breaks over the horizon in the heart of the highlands to reveal a totally unspoilt landscape of rare beauty.

First published in Great Britain in 1984 by The Hamlyn Publishing Group Limited
This edition published in 1989 by Peerage Books
Michelin House, 81 Fulham Road, London SW3 6RB
© The Hamlyn Publishing Group Limited 1984

ISBN 1 85052 131 X
Produced by Mandarin Offset
Printed and bound in Hong Kong

Contents

One of the best restored castles of its kind in Scotland Eilean Donan Castle which lies to the south of the Kyle of Lochalsh was founded in 1230. The view from the rear courtyard is breathtaking.

The Borders

Few lands can have a more spectacular introduction than Scotland, for the Southern Uplands, although dwarfed by their craggy highland counterparts, are no less imposing. It seems almost as if a vast turbulent sea had suddenly solidified and been covered with foliage to create a varied vista of deep green troughs and mountainous peaks. Nestling in their midst are the now tranquil border towns, which in more troubled times were the scene of many bitter and bloody battles.

Gretna. The Auld Smiddy, now sadly idle, remains as a lasting monument to the hundreds of runaway couples who were married there. They fled north to escape the then oppressive English marriage laws which made marriages without parental consent illegal.

Dumfries. An old seaport, one of whose most important industries is now knitwear. It was in the heart of this Royal Burgh that Robert Burns gained the inspiration for some of his most famous songs, including the immortal *Auld Lang Syne* and *Ye Banks and Braes o' Bonny Doon*. A Burns Museum still exists in the house where he died in 1796.

Melrose. It is said that the heart of Robert the Bruce lies in the ruins of the abbey here, reckoned to be one of the finest in Scotland. Built originally in 1136, Melrose Abbey, in common with many others in the area, braved a series of determined attacks by the English before its final destruction in 1544.

Hawick. A border town almost as famous for its rugby as it is for its knitwear. Very little of the old town remains – much of it having been totally destroyed by the English in the raids of 1570, but one remarkably well preserved building now forms part of the Tower Hotel.

Coldstream. A border crossing point used more over the centuries by the warring Scots and English than by tourists. Just three miles from here is the scene of the Battle of Flodden. With an estimated 12,000 casualties on both sides, it was one of the worst battles ever fought on English soil.

Jedburgh. A favourite haunt of Robert Burns and (much earlier) Mary Queen of Scots, Jedburgh, too, has had its share of troubles. The ancient castle here was destroyed, ironically by the Scots themselves, who reckoned it was proving of more use to the English than it was to them.

Kelso. Sir Walter Scott described Kelso as the most beautiful if not the most romantic village in Scotland and it is certainly an ideal touring centre for the Cheviot Hills.

Peebles. Green rolling hills and dense forests surround this picturesque little town, which boasts some of the finest salmon fishing in Scotland. The novelists Robert Louis Stevenson and Samuel Crockett both made their homes here.

Galashiels. A bustling border town noted for its tweeds and its woollens. Every June the history of the town is re-enacted in a colourful pageant to celebrate the anniversary of the granting of its charter in 1599.

Previous page: It is not hard to imagine as you gaze at the impressive structure that was Sir Walter Scott's last and favourite home why he decided to live here. Abbotsford House, where he died in 1832, lies within a fly-cast of the River Tweed and, like the estate that surrounds it, was almost entirely Scott's own creation. The magnificent entrance hall is panelled with wood from the old kirk at Dunfermline and the cornices are clustered with the armorial bearings of the Scottish border families.

The heady perfume of the bonny bloomin' heather wafts gently in the breeze over the softly undulating border hills as an open invitation to ramblers and hill walkers. The Lowther Hills in Dumfriesshire pictured here are a particular favourite with locals and tourists alike. Each hilltop opens up a new and exciting vista of lush green valleys and softly flowing streams.

Opposite page: The tranquil waters of the River Esk meander towards the Solway Firth near Canonbie. An area of land between the rivers Esk and Sark was the subject of many bitter disputes between the Scots and the English leading it to be known as 'Debatable Land'. Those who lived in it had to fight for the privilege.

Left: The dramatic sight of the Grey Mare's Tail lies to the north east of Moffat on the main Selkirk road. The waters plunge some 200 feet from the isolated Loch Skene to join Moffat Water and were once described by Scott in *Marmion* as 'white as the snowy charger's tail'.

Below: This spectacular steep-sided hollow known as the Devil's Beef Tub lies off the A701 some five miles outside Moffat. Once used by cattle thieves to hide their ill-gotten gains it also saved the life of a young Jacobite who was captured at Culloden in 1746. For as the English were escorting him to Carlisle and certain death he leapt over the side and scrambled down the steep slopes to safety.

Top left: Surely one of the best known sights in the country, the 'auld smiddy' at Gretna Green now lies sadly idle, although thousands of visitors every year still flock to see the ancient anvil where runaway couples were wed. Their romantic excursions north of the border were made necessary in 1754 with the introduction of an English law which prohibited couples marrying without their parents' consent. No such embargo existed to shackle the emotions of the warm-hearted Scots and for almost 200 years marriage ceremonies were carried out here.

Centre left: The dramatic six-arched structure of Devorguilla's Bridge casts its impressive shadow over the Nith in the heart of Dumfries. Built in the 13th

century by Lady Devorguilla, who also founded the nearby New Abbey, it is now used only by pedestrians.

Bottom left: One of Scotland's best preserved stately homes, the magnificent Drumlanrig Castle is a seat of the Duke of Buccleuch. Its impressive salmon-pink exterior and lavish furnishings make it a regular haunt for visitors and there is an excellent woodland play area for children in its grounds. Built between 1676 and 1689 the cost of it so horrified the first Duke of Queensberry that he spent only one night in it. The former Douglas stronghold is still packed with fine art treasures including a Rembrandt original.

Above: It is not hard to see why Scott waxed so lyrical about the borders. One of his favourite haunts, aptly called Scott's View lies just off the B6356 near Melrose and affords breathtaking views over the Tweed to the Eildon Hills. Scott spent so much of his time here that it is said that horses drawing his hearse to Dryburgh Abbey stopped here of their own accord to afford his soul a last glance at his best-loved lands. From the highest of the three summits of the Eildon Hills Scott claimed he could point out 'forty-three places famous in war and verse'.

Scotland has long been justifiably proud of her impressive geological heritage and sights like this, off the 300-feet high red sandstone cliffs at St Abbs Head are common all round the coast. Time and tide have taken their toll over the centuries to sculpt the age-old rock into a massive yet slowly changing tapestry of beauty. The salty sea stacks pictured here are best seen from the winding coastal path that hugs the shoreline from the quaint little fishing village of St Abbs itself two miles to the south. Today the cliffs provide a scenic spectacle for the rambling tourist but in days gone by the watery caves at their foot were a regular haunt of smugglers and vagabonds.

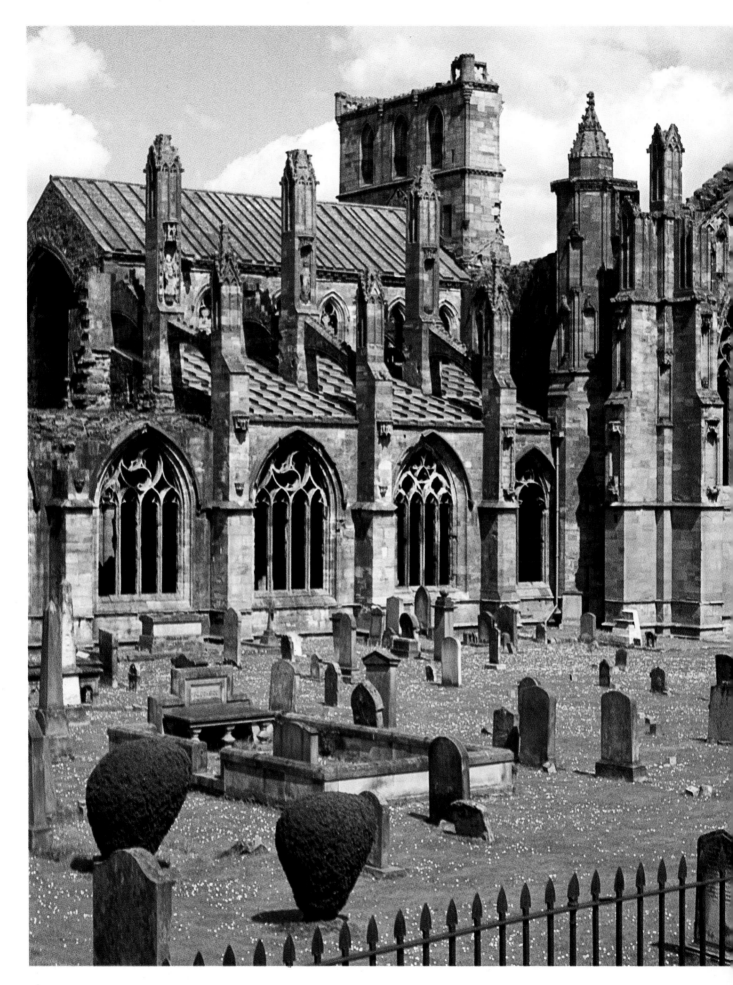

Left: Built originally in 1136 by David I for Cistercian monks Melrose Abbey remains one of the finest of its kind in Scotland. Its present condition is remarkable considering the series of damaging English raids it suffered in the 14th and 16th centuries. The remains of the stone vaultings are impressively elaborate and remain as a lasting tribute to the tremendous skill and flair of the traditional Scottish stone carvers. The east window of five lights divided by a cross transom with its 'slender shafts of shapely stone' is flatteringly described in Scott's

The Lay of the Last Minstrel and it is said that the heart of Robert the Bruce lies interred immediately beneath it. In 1921 excavations revealed the full ground plan of the cloisters and identified many parts of the monastic buildings. In a corner of the graveyard is a red stone erected by Sir Walter Scott himself to mark the grave of his favourite henchman Tom Purdie, who died in 1829.

Above: No visit to Scott's country would be complete without a visit to his last and most famous home in Abbotsford. The many-turreted mansion still contains many of his favoured historical relics. A glass case contains the last suit of clothes worn by Scott and his well-stocked library houses a collection of almost 20,000 rare books. The bust on the fireplace, done by Chantry in 1820, is considered to be the best likeness of Scott. It is said that when Scott died in 1832 his bed had been put near a window in the dining room within sight of the River Tweed.

Right: Near the heart of the border town of Jedburgh is Queen Mary's House where Mary Queen of Scots almost died from exhaustion after riding to visit Bothwell at Hermitage Castle in 1566. Today it is a museum containing the Queen's death mask and her Communion set – and an ancient watch belonging to the Queen which was found in a bog outside the town some 200 years after her death.

Below: The old abbey dates from 1150. Like its counterpart at Melrose the abbey suffered gravely at the hands of the English but much of the main arcade with its clustered pillars remains. Constructed of old red sandstone much of the 86-feet high tower was rebuilt in 1500 and the choir, although now only of two bays, is still largely intact.

Far right: Attractively set by the River Tweed in the heart of the Tweedale Hills Peebles is justifiably proud of its reputation as a haven for sportsmen. Wooded hills provide a backdrop for some of the finest angling in the area and there is a splendid eighteen-hole golf course.

Glasgow and
The Firth of Clyde

Although the scenery here is less spectacular than farther north the gently rolling hills of the Clyde valley have a splendour all of their own. The coastal regions particularly, with their fine sands and seaside resorts, remain a firm favourite with Scottish and foreign holidaymakers alike, and there are many places of historical interest.

Glasgow. A much maligned but much changed city. Architecturally there is little to beat it in Scotland and its former reputation as a haunt for razor gangs has now all but vanished. Glasgow boasts one of the finest urban road developments in Europe, permitting rapid and comfortable travel throughout the city and its environs. Less than five minutes from the city centre the sprawling acres of Pollok Estate offer a country-like haven for city dwellers and contain two superb art galleries. In the heart of Glasgow itself the Museum, Art Gallery, and University are notable buildings.

Tignabruich. Some of the most pleasing views of the western lowland coast are afforded from this picturesque little village nestling on the Kyles of Bute. The drive there, across the Cowal peninsula, offers many breathtaking sights and the pleasant ferry journey from Gourock to Dunoon over the Firth of Clyde puts it within easy reach of the main centres of population.

Arrochar. Situated at the foot of some of Argyll's finest mountains, Arrochar stands at the head of Loch Long. The narrow wooded road from Helensburgh skirts the lochside for almost its entire length and the shores of Loch Lomond are a mere two miles away.

Alloway. The birthplace of Robert Burns: the tiny thatched cottage where he was born in 1759 has been preserved and is now open to the public. The Auld Brig, immortalized in the poem *Tam o' Shanter*, was reckoned to have been built in the 13th century and still spans the Doon.

Ayr. Situated in the heart of Burns country Ayr, with its fine beaches and attractive fishing harbour, is a popular tourist resort. John Macadam, the man who invented modern road surfaces, was born here.

Culzean Castle. This lies an easy drive south on the coastal road from Ayr. Built in the late 18th century and incorporating a medieval keep, the castle and its finely laid-out gardens are now open to the public.

Largs. A pleasing seaside resort with much to attract the sporting fraternity. Its well-used pier makes an excellent starting point for trips to the Kyles of Bute and the Clyde islands, and some of the finest fish and chips in the country can be found in the series of seafood restaurants that line the windswept promenade.

Dunoon. A popular resort for fishermen and yachtsmen, Dunoon is also host to the picturesque and colourful Cowal Highland Games in July each year.

Campbeltown. Former Beatle Paul McCartney, who sang the praises of the Mull of Kintyre, still lives near this charming little fishing town. Machrihanish, with its fine golf course, is nearby.

Previous page: Situated in the heart of the hilly Cowal country Loch Fyne is one of the largest and best known of Scottish sea lochs. Famous for its fine herrings it is also a favoured yachting centre and tourist spot. It is, perhaps, best seen from its northernmost tip where the lofty peaks of Beinn Bhuide and Beinn an Lochain reach for the sky.

In common with many British rivers the Clyde has been substantialy cleaned up in recent years and yachting even in the west coast's blustery conditions is pursued with considerable enthusiasm.

Above: Scotland may be better known for its scenic splendour than its fascinating foliage but the latter is no less remarkable. Indeed throughout the climatically mild west coast sub-tropical and even tropical plants abound. The temperate waters of the Gulf Stream, which originate in the Caribbean, are largely responsible for this. Some of the western isles have virtually never known freezing temperatures and in some sheltered shores tropical agriculture is almost native. The old walled Logan Gardens are a fine example. Sadly much of the north-west coast of England is deprived of the benevolent effect of the stream by the intervention of Ireland but in the far north near Poolewe a public garden boasts the largest Magnolia tree in existence and a 50-foot hydrangea.

Right: Culzean Castle with its multi-turreted façade remains a lasting testimony to the great Robert Adam who built it for the 10th Earl of Cassilis in 1777. Now open to the public it contains many fascinating relics of days past. A little known fact is that in 1946 the top flat of the castle was given to General Eisenhower as his Scottish residence. The immaculately maintained gardens offer a splendid view over the broadening Firth of Clyde to the Isle of Arran. Nearby there is the amazing 'electric brae' where cars, through an optical illusion, appear to freewheel uphill!

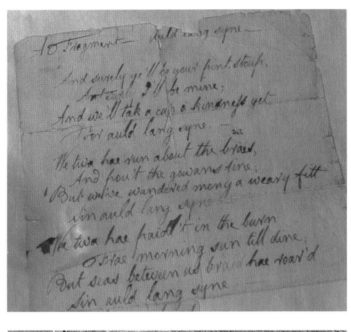

Far left: The auld bard himself immortalized this seemingly unprepossessing piece of architecture in his famous poem *Tam o' Shanter.* It was here, at the Brig o' Doon, according to Robert Burns, that the braw grey mare Meg had her tail pulled off as she fled the supernatural spirits that sought the soul of her master Tam. As Burns, and legend, would have it the witches who chased his legendary hero dare not cross running water and so the single arched 13th-century bridge that still spans the River Doon became Tam's salvation. I still have remarkable respect for the English RAF officer at Abingdon who, at a Burns night, recited the entire poem without reference to notes. I can only imagine that he must have followed the same picturesque route as Tam.

Top left: Nearby, at Alloway, is the birthplace of the bard himself. The old thatched cottage, built up from a clay biggin by the poet's father, was later transformed into a pub but as a mark of respect to Burns it has now been restored as his original abode.

Centre left: Now a museum, the old cottage contains many interesting relics, including Burns's original manuscript of the internationally-known *Auld Lang Syne.*

Bottom left: A little farther south lies the village of Kirkoswald where two of Burns's best known characters, Tam o' Shanter, and Souter Johnnie, lie buried in the churchyard, along with the body of Burns's own father who died in 1784. Here, at Souter Johnnie's former cottage, stand life-sized stone carvings of many of the poet's characters.

Opposite, top left: The much maligned city of Glasgow has changed. The impressive façade of Pollok House, built in 1752 by William Adam, is a mere three miles from the heart of the city yet is set in the midst of one of the finest public parklands in Europe. Originally the home of the Maxwells of Pollok, the house and the acres of woodland that surround it were gifted to the city as recently as 1967. Today the house contains the Stirling Maxwell collection of Spanish paintings including works by Greco and Goya and the old Edwardian kitchen, now faithfully restored, serves teas and lunches to visitors. Nearby the newly constructed art gallery to house the Burrell Art Collection has recently opened. But the art treasures are not centred wholly on the outskirts. In the Hunterian Museum and Art Gallery (*top right*) there are significant collections in geology, archaeology, anthropology and numismatics. The Charles Rennie Mackintosh room is contained in the Art Gallery in Hillhead Street.

Opposite, bottom: The city chambers in George Square have been at the forefront of many Glaswegian changes, not least their own. The rather grubby exterior was transformed when the stonework was cleaned and the splendid 19th-century structure is one of the city's architectural highlights.

Left: Kibble Palace in Glasgow's Botanic Gardens remains one of the most impressive hothouses for plants in the world. Originally built as a huge private conservatory for John Kibble at his Clyde coast home near Loch Long it was dismantled, transported, and rebuilt on its present site in the up-market suburb of Kelvinside in 1873. Originally intended to serve as a concert hall and meeting place it now hosts a variety of plants and trees from all over the world.

Top left: The colour and pageantry of a fully-fledged Highland Games is not to be missed and the famous Cowal Highland Gathering at Dunoon at the end of August is reckoned to be one of the best in Scotland. Perhaps the most impressive and moving sight comes even before the games begin as hundreds of pipers from all over the world pack the tiny ferries that plough backwards and forwards from Gourock to the Cowal Peninsula. The haunting melodies that float across the Firth of Clyde are unforgettable.

Left: The imposing silhouette of Brodick Castle overlooks the town of the same name on the holiday isle of Arran. Parts of it date back to the 14th century and until 1957 it was the ancestral mansion of the Hamiltons. Set in impressive woodland gardens of more than 60 acres the castle contains some fine watercolours by Rowlandson and some excellent Turner landscapes.

The brightly lit esplanade of Rothesay at night has been a welcome sight for many weary travellers in the past. One of the most popular tourist resorts on the Clyde it lies at the head of a fine bay commanding beautiful views over the Firth. An ancient royal burgh, its now ruined castle dates back to the 12th century. It was invaded by Norsemen in 1230, took further punishment in the Civil War, and was eventually burned by a brother of the Earl of Argyll in 1685. At the nearby High Kirk it is said that the bodies of five 14th-century bishops lie buried.

The picturesque village of
Arrochar lies in the heart of
Macfarlane country and makes an
ideal touring centre. Just two
miles to the east lie the romantic
shores of Loch Lomond and to
the west the long slow climb up
the 'Rest and be Thankful' is
more than adequately rewarded
with the view from the top. The
long steep incline up Glen Croe
has been known as the 'Rest and
Be Thankful' since a stone with
that inscription was placed on the
old road when it was being
repaired by the army in the 18th
century. Wordsworth at least
regarded the advice as superfluous
asking 'Who . . . rests not
thankful?' To the south, as
previously described, a narrow
winding road skirts the lochside
to the larger resort of
Helensburgh.

Edinburgh and
The East Coast

If variety be the spice of life then those who seek it would be well advised to explore this region thoroughly. From the cultured capital to the tiny fishing villages that adorn the eastern extremities there is something here for everyone, including St Andrews with its golf and Perth, notable for whisky distilling. Much of Scotland's lucrative fishing industry lies along these shores and oil, the black gold from the sea bed, has brought boom times and, regrettably, boom prices to areas like Aberdeen. Hunting, fishing, shooting, and skiing are all readily available here, a fact not ignored by royalty who are frequent visitors to these parts.

Edinburgh. Scotland's capital since 1437, this civilized, beautiful, and clean city has struggled hard to become what it is today. It was at one time a cesspit of violence, dirt, and disease, but its standing has steadily improved in more recent times. The once dingy Royal Mile has now been admirably restored and its narrow cobbled streets lead directly to the imposing castle which overlooks the city. Nearby, the extinct volcano, Arthur's Seat, offers another splendid viewpoint for sightseers. The impressive botanical gardens are at their most beautiful in spring and summer and the collection of paintings at the National Gallery is reckoned to be one of the finest in Scotland.

Perth. Sir Walter Scott wrote, 'Amid all the provinces of Scotland, if an intelligent stranger were asked to describe the most varied and the most beautiful, it is probable he could name the county of Perth . . .' The fair city itself, a former capital, is equal to that praise. Built at the head of the famous salmon river Tay, it makes an ideal touring centre for central Scotland. Three first-class golf courses add to its considerable attractions.

St Andrews. Home of the Royal and Ancient and, many would say, golf itself. Once the ecclesiastical centre for the whole of Scotland, it also boasts the country's oldest university, which was founded in 1412. Excellent trout fishing is to be found nearby and the town has several popular, and safe, beaches.

Crail. A delightful spot for a leisurely lunch or an overnight stay, this picturesque fishing village has a dark and ominous past. Once the haunt of smugglers and vagabonds who sought shelter and seclusion

Previous page: The impressive skyline of Scotland's capital at night. Though many museums and places of interest are closed after dark the famous Rose Street with its wide and varied collection of public houses and restaurants is well worth a visit.

The sleek yet strong outlines of the two Forth Bridges remain a lasting testimony to the skill and dedication of Scotland's engineers. Sir Benjamin Baker built the impressive 2,765-yard railway bridge between 1883 and 1890. The 2,000-yard road bridge was completed in 1964.

along the craggy shores, it is now more noted for its peace and tranquillity.

Arbroath. Home of the famous 'smokies', haddock browned and smoked over an oak fire, this is where Scotland's Declaration of Independence was signed by Robert the Bruce in 1320. A popular seaside resort with fine beaches, it is also a favourite with sea anglers.

Aberdeen. The granite city that became a boom town. House prices here are among the highest in Britain, and the houses themselves among the strongest built. The third largest town in Scotland, it is still an important fishing port and the loving attention lavished on its many acres of parkland and gardens make it one of the most attractive cities in the country.

Carnoustie. Boasts one of the finest championship golf courses in the world. Its popular sandy beaches and other sporting amenities make it an ideal spot for all the family.

Above: The dark, gloomy, spiral staircase in the former Royal Palace at Linlithgow has known many a famous footfall. James V was born here as was his daughter Mary Queen of Scots. Queen Margaret sought solace in its darkened rooms as she vainly awaited the return of her husband James IV from Flodden and Henry VI of England is said to have taken refuge within its walls. Although from the outside the castle looks somewhat bleak and unappealing the inner quadrangle features some fascinating examples of 15th-century sculpture. Nearby the famous St Michael's church is reckoned to be one of the finest in Scotland.

Right: Situated at the end of the Royal Mile in Edinburgh the Palace of Holyrood House is the chief Royal Palace in Scotland. The home of Mary Queen of Scots for six tragic years it is still an official Royal residence. Work on the massive French-style structure was begun in 1500 by James IV and it was completed in its first state by James V before being all but razed to the ground by the Earl of Hertford's men in 1544. The Historical Apartments on the first floor include the impressive picture gallery which features the portraits of no less than 111 Scottish monarchs who, according to Sir Walter Scott, 'if they ever existed lived several hundred years before the invention of oil painting'.

Top left: Thousands of tourists are attracted to Edinburgh every year by the impressive military tattoo held at the ancient castle. Special stands are set up round the battlements to ensure that everyone can share the splendour of the spectacle. There can be few more moving moments than those at the close when a lone piper plays his soulful lament beneath the floodlights.

Centre left: The lush gardens between Edinburgh's Princes' Street provide a verdant green foreground for the castle itself.

Bottom left: Knox, whose house is pictured here, led the Protestant Reformation in Scotland in the 16th century. The house is thought to have been built by the goldsmith to Mary Queen of Scots. Opposite the house there is a childhood museum with an

interesting collection of children's memorabilia.

Above: One of the finest views of the city is from the 350-feet high Calton Hill. In the foreground you can see Charles Cockerell's Parthenon – a monument to the Scots who fell in the Napoleonic campaigns.

Above right: The tightly clustered buildings of Whitehorse Close

were the original starting point for the London mail coach. It is said that the Jacobite leaders assembled here before meeting their fate in the 1745 rebellion.

Right: The impressive Victorian balustrade at Victoria Terrace overlooks Edinburgh's ancient Grassmarket – for over a century a place of execution. Today it is more famous for its antique shops and the Traverse Theatre.

Above left: The 400-year-old Preston Mill situated off the road between East Linton and Tyninghame is still in pristine condition thanks to the National Trust. Originally established by monks from a nearby monastery the restored mill is still capable of producing more than 22,000

pounds of meal an hour. It rarely
does so, however, the machinery
grinding more slowly these days
to illustrate the intricate workings
of the old-fashioned machinery.

Left: The well preserved
Dunnottar Castle stands on a
rocky promontory 160 feet above

the sea near the Montrose road.
Although the gatehouse, built
around 1575, was said to be the
strongest in Scotland, it could not
withstand the notorious onslaught
during the Wars of the
Commonwealth. Fortunately a
quick-thinking Minister's wife
was able to safeguard Scotland's

Crown Jewels by smuggling
them through the very enemy
that threatened them. In 1685 the
dungeon imprisoned more than
150 Covenanters and it was the
headstone of their graves that
'Old Mortality' was cleaning
when Scott visited him in the
nearby churchyard.

The impressive Bass Rock is the
best known of the rocky islets
that lie off Scotland's eastern
coast. The precipitous, 350-feet
high mass of basalt is the home of
thousands of sea birds, mostly
gannets. A castle once stood here
and traces of its old fortifications
can still be seen. After 1671 the
island was also used as a prison
for Covenanters.

The creak of timbers and the odour of creosote prevail in the functional, yet picturesque harbour of Crail on the Fife coast. The gently-lapping waters of the North Sea can seem deceptively timid under a blue summer sky, but the angry gales that lash the colourful coastline in winter are awesome. The little cluster of red-roofed 17th-century houses that surround the harbour were a traditional haunt of smugglers and vagabonds. Today, more interest is taken in them by aspiring artists. The old toll-house, built in the early 16th century, sports a gilded salmon on its weathervane and a coat of arms dated 1602. Nearby lie the famous caves of Caiplie, some of which are more than 30 feet long. They have been well used by smugglers in the past.

46

Right: Few Scottish regiments can have a more notable past than the Black Watch. Their exploits are recorded at a museum in Perth housed in the imposing Balhousie Castle, the regimental headquarters since 1962.

Below: If Scotland be the home of golf then St Andrew's is its royal castle. But this charming seaside town is more than a sporting haven. Standing on a rocky promontory it also houses Scotland's oldest university, and in summer is a fashionable and much-used tourist spot.

Far right: The setting for a tragedy by Britain's greatest playright. As you walk through the imposing front hall of Glamis Castle in Tayside, it is not hard to imagine the presence of Macbeth, with murder in his heart. Steeped in history, the ancestral home of the Earl of Strathmore was rebuilt in the 17th century in the style of a French château. The Queen Mother spent her childhood at Glamis and Princess Margaret was born here.

Far left: Tall ships stand proudly in Aberdeeen's ancient harbour. Traditionally the centre of Scotland's lucrative fishing industry Aberdeen is now also the oil capital of the country. The city, with its cathedral and university, is built almost entirely from local granite and the architecture is unique. The 'northern lights' are a frequent and awesome sight in these parts.

Left: To the north of Aberdeen, and in the centre of its own well-tended gardens lies Crathes Castle. The double square tower was completed in 1596. A jewelled ivory horn, said to have belonged to Robert the Bruce, is preserved in the main hall.

Below: Built around 1520 by the Bishop Gavin Dunbar the Bridge of Dee consists of seven ribbed arches each inscribed with various coats of arms.

Above: Few people associate Scotland with culinary delicacies yet the country's local produce provides many rare and unparalleled dishes. Better salmon, either smoked or fresh, can rarely be found and for centuries the Scots have been justifiably proud of their high quality beef. Crabs, lobsters, prawns, and other shellfish abound off the coast and where else in Britain could you buy a one-pound lobster, cooked as you like it, for just £3 in 1984? But there are other less well-known

delicacies like the highly-flavoured slicing sausage, the Arbroath smokies (smoked haddock), the unique breakfast rolls, and the fantastic soups that still form part of the staple diet of all Scots. The celebrated haggis can even be bought in fish-and-chip shops where the old-fashioned fish supper (fish and chips – served in a newspaper of course) is a delicacy indeed. Strangely Scotland is also famed for the quality of its Indian Restaurants some of the best of which are in Glasgow's Gibson

Street (including the Shish Mahal and the Koh-i-Noor).

Top right: But if there is a true taste of Scotland then it must be in its whisky, undoubtedly the finest in the world. Although there are some 2,000 different brands, more than 150 of them single malts, great care, and pride, goes into the production of every bottle. The giant stills pictured here perform just one of the many essential processes necessary for the production of a proper whisky. Many of the processes

remain a closely-guarded secret amongst the distillers whose intense rivalry ensures the superior quality of their product.

Right: The long and intricate distilling procedures are now over and the final product is bottled.

Far right: But as it flows constant checks are being carried out by dedicated testers who can spot a fault simply by smelling the bouquet.

53

Loch Lomond and
The Trossachs

Nature must have been at its most benevolent when it came to bestowing beauty on this particular part of Scotland. It is remarkable what striking geographical contrasts are to be found in so limited an area. At almost every bend in the road a new and breathtaking vista unfolds, giving the visitor a true insight into the remarkable unspoilt beauty of the Southern Highlands. Most routes are narrow and winding, but to travel at speed through such awesome scenery would be sacrilege. Rivers, lochs, and mountains combine to provide a feast of fantastic splendour for the eye. This may be the smallest region covered in the book, but for scenery it is, perhaps, the best. As the Scots say, 'Guid gear goes intae sma' bulk' – good things come in small packages.

Loch Lomond. The largest and possibly the most famous of all the Scottish lochs, it more than does justice to the flattering lyrics that describe its bonny banks. The trunk road that runs up the western shores is one of the main access roads to the Highlands and the far north, and the views afforded from it as it twists and winds along the loch's contours are breathtaking. As you look across the deep waters of the loch to the opposite shore the majestic peak of Ben Lomond can be seen piercing the clouds.

On the opposite side of the loch the pretty single-track road meanders through Drymen, and Balmaha to Rowardennan, where it comes to an abrupt halt at the foot of the great mountain. A regular steamer service stops at such picturesque harbours as Luss, Rowardennan, and Inversnaid.

Callander. Frequented often by Sir Walter Scott, Callander remains a major resort and is ideally situated as a touring centre for the Trossachs. Known as the gateway to the Highlands, it has a splendid 18-hole golf course. Game, coarse fishing, water skiing and sailing are all available nearby.

Luss. A tiny but beautiful village right on the shores of Loch Lomond. The single narrow street, bordered by ancient stone cottages, leads right down to the pier. Local crafts are on sale in a number of shops and in the summer the local Highland Games provide a colourful spectacle.

Lochearnhead. Lies at the head of the picturesque Loch Earn which is widely used and ideally suited for water sports. Another Higland Games venue, it also offers fine opportunities for hill walking. To the southeast the lofty peaks of Ben Vorlich, 3224 feet, and Stuc a' Chroin, provide a spectacular backdrop to the loch.

Balloch. Lies at the foot of Loch Lomond and can be reached by motorway from the centre of Glasgow in half an hour. Britain's first bear park is situated here and a wide variety of boats can be hired for trips on the loch itself.

Crianlarich. At the northernmost tip of the loch, Crianlarich has become an important centre for hill walkers and not too ambitious climbers.

Loch Katrine. This beautiful reservoir – it provides much of Glasgow's water – was the inspiration for Scott's poem *The Lady of the Lake*. A steamer trip on the loch or a walk through the dramatic Pass of Achraig will afford the visitor splendid views impossible to enjoy from the road.

Aberfoyle. A pleasant little village nestling in a delightful woodland setting just south of the Achray Forest. Nearby, at Loch Ard, are the two waterfalls described in Scott's *Waverley*.

Previous page: There can be few more enjoyable ways of taking in the delightful Trossachs scenery than astride a trusty trekking pony. Gently nursing you through scenes that no car driver and only the fittest hillwalkers may have seen they are perhaps the best guides to this wonderland of natural beauty. There are several trekking centres in the area offering one to seven-day excursions, and little expertise is needed to master the leisurely art of follow my leader on horseback.

Right: Alternatively the steamer that ploughs the waters of Loch Lomond is another way of getting an unusual insight into the surroundings. Tarbet Pier, pictured opposite, is one of many jumping-off points for pleasure cruises on the loch. By planning your day in advance you could easily have a leisurely lunch and an afternoon ramble before rejoining the steamer for the trip back to your starting point.

Above: The bonny banks and bonny braes of Loch Lomond have made it internationally famous. No monsters are said to lurk in its depths and nor has it a dark and mysterious past. Its popularity lies in the simple fact that with the surrounding hills it combines to present some of the finest scenery in the country. It is even more remarkable to consider as you look across the loch to Ben Lomond that half-an-hour's drive away almost a million people live and work in a big city. Many a wry comment has been made in the past about Glasgow, with would-be wits claiming the best thing the city had to offer was the road out – but if that road be the A82 which meanders along the western shores of Loch Lomond then it is hard to fault their assertions. The scenery here has inspired poets and songwriters alike. Thousands flock to these beautiful shores every year yet the area remains unspoilt and largely uncommercialized. Indeed, much of the eastern shore can only be reached on foot.

Top right: One of the best ways of viewing the impressive scenery, without the distractions of driving, is on the *Maid of the Loch.* The old steamer stops at a number of lochside piers enabling visitors to fully explore this delightful area.

Centre right: Many choose to spend some time at the picturesque village of Luss where a variety of small shops offer an almost bewildering choice of local crafts and items of interest. The short walk from the pier to the local hotel for lunch is a well trodden one.

Bottom right: Many who explore the region stay at the Lomond Castle Hotel a few miles north of Balloch. The restaurant and bar windows overlook the loch and a comprehensive menu, featuring many traditional dishes, is available. In the gardens are a number of Swiss-style chalets offering self-catering accommodation within a stone's throw of the loch. A new leisure centre was opened in the spring of 1984.

Above: Winter stretches its frosty finger over the bonny banks of little Loch Lubnaig in the heart of the Trossachs. Although there is not much of this pretty loch to enjoy – it stretches for only some 4 miles alongside the A84 – the roadside views are magnificent. Nearby a tiny churchyard marks the site of St Bride's Chapel where according to Scott's *The Lady of the Lake* a fiery cross was thrust into the hands of a young Norman on his wedding day.

Right: The morning mist rolls over the foothills of the aptly named 'Rest And Be Thankful' to the west of Arrochar. The popular A83 which rises to some 1,000 feet is the main trunk road to the Mull of Kintyre with all its romantic associations. Were such a fine and gently sloping road available to the army when they were working on the old road the hill might never have been called the 'Rest and be Thankful'.

Far left: One of the most picturesque stretches of water in Scotland, Loch Katrine is also one of the most functional, serving as it does much of the Greater Glasgow area with its water supply. Much of the scenery surrounding the loch is unspoilt even by road and the best way of seeing it is either on foot, or on one of the regular boat trips round the loch. Stretching for some nine miles through the spendour of the Trossachs Loch Katrine must be one of the most beautiful of all reservoirs.

Left: The impressive bronze statue of Robert the Bruce overlooks the scene of the bloody battle of Bannockburn, near Stirling. Unveiled by the Queen in 1964 it commemorated the 650th anniversary of the battle where inferior Scottish forces won their independence through a series of secret strategies.

Below: On the outskirts of the beautiful town of Stirling stands its imposing castle. Now substantially restored the castle was first built in the 12th century and later became a royal residence.

The Central Highlands

Previous page: The bleak and barren landscape around the Black Mount, to the north of the Bridge of Orchy is chilling even in summer, but in winter arctic comparisons are easy to draw. The main road, which continues north through the pass of Glencoe follows the eastern contours of these rugged moors.

It is appropriate that the highest mountain range in Britain should also host the finest winter sports facilities. Every year thousands flock to the craggy slopes of the Cairngorms (nine peaks top 4,000 feet) for their skiing pleasure. Cairn Gorm itself has the most accessible summit with a chairlift

taking visitors most of the way there. The largest nature reserve in Britain lies in the heart of this isolated countryside and access to most of it is unrestricted. Summer temperatures here can plummet alarmingly and local advice should be taken before rambling or hill walking.

If one thing is to be learnt from the barren terrain that dominates in this part of the country it is that man must take second place to nature, for it is here that some of the bleakest and most forlorn sights in Britain can be seen. Nature may have been generous when it bestowed scenic beauty on the Highlands – it was also merciless. Every year climbers and hill walkers, lured by the deceptively easy-looking ascents and apparently fair weather, venture into the hillsides. Although there are comparatively few fatalities, many owe their lives to the selfless efforts of the mountain rescue teams. However, with care and with expert advice there is no reason why the visitor cannot enjoy the full range of sporting facilities this area has to offer, including climbing, hill walking, fishing, hunting, shooting, and stalking. There are many impressive sights to be seen but few more chilling than the views across the almost lunar landscape of Rannoch Moor on a stormy day. Miles upon miles of heather-clad moor seem to stretch endlessly into the distance without a sign of habitation or life. Moreover, the imposing and almost frightening experience of the Pass Of Glencoe on a similar day can leave no one untouched.

Fort William. Famed as a touring centre for the West Highlands, this busy little market town lies at the foot of Ben Nevis, at 4406 feet the tallest mountain in Britain. Each year hardened athletes compete in a race to the summit and back again but for the less hardy there are clearly marked walking routes to the top, which affords splendid views.

Inverness. Straddling the picturesque River Ness, this pretty town, dubbed the capital of the Highlands, is one of the most attractive in Scotland. It is the last stop on the longest train journey in Britain (568 mi. from London) and is still widely recognized as the major communications and administration centre for the Highlands. The fishing around here is excellent and the town also boasts an eighteen-hole golf course. The impressive castle which stands on Castle Hill is well worth a visit.

Loch Ness. The deep and dark waters of the loch still hold the secret of the monster. Tales of mysterious beings and fearsome creatures being seen

here date back to the seventh century when an abbot claimed to have prevented the monster from eating a friend. Since then, of course, there have been many alleged sightings, but despite the numerous scientific surveys and the constant presence of the amateur hunters no one has yet substantiated the existence of Nessie. The loch itself is more than 700 feet deep in places and forms part of the great chain of lochs that splits Scotland from Fort William to Inverness.

Pitlochry. Another ideal tourist centre with a wealth of small and hospitable hotels for the weary traveller. The dam which lies to the west of the town, includes a spectacular fish pass where lively salmon can be seen battling upstream in the spring. Fishing throughout this areas is as excellent as it is varied and the town boasts two golf courses, one 18-hole and one 9-hole. The picturesque falls of Tummel are close by, situated in the heart of the magnificent Tummel Valley.

Balmoral Castle. Still used by members of the royal family, this fine example of Scottish baronial architecture was at one time bought for just £31,000. Included in the price paid by the Prince Consort in 1850 was the entire estate. Tiny Crathie Church, the royal family's official place of worship when in residence, stands nearby.

Killiecrankie. The scene of yet another bloody battle, in which the supporters of James II of England defeated the forces of William III. Ironically, the man who won the battle for James, Viscount Dundee, was killed at the moment of victory.

Aviemore. In the early 1960s Aviemore was little more than a hamlet on the main A9 road to Inverness. Today it is the biggest and the most modern tourist centre in the North. Although sometimes criticized for being over-commercialized, it does provide all the facilities necessary for the family holiday. Situated in the heart of the beautiful Cairngorms, the sporting facilities include ice-skating, curling, go-kart racing, pony trekking, hill walking, mountaineering, skiing, and many more, and there is a wealth of reasonably priced self-catering and hotel accommodation.

Above: The 'three sisters' of Glencoe stamp their imposing and unequivocal presence over the glen. The lofty peaks of Beinn Fhada, Gearr Aonach, and Aonach Dubh, each rises more than 2,500 feet above sea level, and forms part of the massive wall of rock that hems in the narrow pass. It was here in 1692, ironically on February the 13th, that the horrific massacre took place. The alleged cause of the slaughter was the failure of Macdonald of Glencoe to swear his allegiance to the King. As a result a troop of soldiers, led by Robert Campbell of Glen Lyon converged on the darkened glen at dawn to butcher some 40 men, women, and children. In fact it is said that Macdonald had already pledged his allegiance. Having left it to the last moment he found no one of competence in Fort William to record it and was forced to travel further afield to Inverary. When the papers arrived in Edinburgh a few days later the damage had already been done. The order for the massacre was, according to legend, written on a playing card, the nine of diamonds, which, to this day, is known as the 'Curse of Scotland'. The main road through Glencoe, also known as the Glen of Weeping, rises to 1,000 feet affording magnificent views.

Right: Another view across the Glen featuring the local mountain rescue post. It is here that the hardened professionals that make up the mountain rescue team maintain their constant vigil over their terrain. Thousands of hill walkers and mountaineers ascend the steep slopes every year without incident but in winter the hillsides can be treacherous and many heroic rescues have been co-ordinated through this post.

At 4,406 feet the lofty summit of
Ben Nevis stands head and
shoulders above all the other
mountains in Britain. Its nearest
rival, Snowdon, is a mere 3,560
feet. Ben Nevis can hardly be
described as a graceful mountain
and since there is no apparent
peak or cone at the top its
tremendous size is not
immediately obvious but anyone
who has climbed the summit can
testify to every foot. The ascent
itself it not that arduous and
indeed every year a group of
dedicated athletes take part in a
race to the top and back. Glen
Nevis, one of the loveliest in
Scotland, lies around the giant
mountain's south and west flanks
with the beautiful wooded gorge
of the River Nevis at the far end.
The Ben itself can be climbed
from Achintree Farm some two
and a half miles from Fort
William on the east bank of the
river. A reasonably fit hill walker
can be expected to reach the
sumit in around four hours; it
takes slightly less time coming
down. Nearby, and just to the
north of Spean Bridge on the
main Inverness Road, lies the
beautiful Loch Lochy. A
charming family-owned hotel,
the Letterfinlay Lodge, stands on
its shores and offers a wide
variety of home-cooked local
produce in its restaurant.

Above left: The Falls of Dochart near where the fast flowing rivers of Dochart and Lochay meet just outside Killin in Perthshire. Near the 18th-century Dochart bridge are two small islands, one of them being the former burial ground of the clan McNab. Killin is an all the year round resort offering local angling in the summer and skiing in the winter.

Left: A series of locks at Fort Augustus allow the passage of pleasure boats through Scotlands' Great Glen and down the lovely Caledonian Canal. The Great Glen is a gigantic rift valley that splits Scotland in two from Inverness in the east to the Atlantic in the west and it is completely navigable. It took more than 40 years of dedicated engineering by Thomas Telford before the canal was finally opened in 1847 but it has been a source of pleasure to thousands since. There are 29 locks in all linking the picturesque lochs of Ness, Oich, Lochy, and Linnhe. One of the most spectacular sights is at Corpach where a series of eight locks raise the water level an amazing sixty four feet. Work on the mammoth structure was begun in 1805 but it was not until almost twenty years later that the locks were finally opened amid tremendous celebrations. The corespondent of the *Inverness Courier* lost count of the toasts after 32 and confessed: 'we cannot pretend to detail of the proceedings of the evening.'

Above: The deep and dark waters of Loch Ness have still not yielded their best-kept secret and Nessie, if she exists, does so in splendid seclusion. Loch Ness, which extends from Inverness to Fort Augustus, is more than 700 feet deep in places and her chilly waters have never been known to freeze. Numerous expeditions have been launched since the first report of strange creatures here around the 7th century but no proof of weird creatures has yet been found.

The Battle of Culloden was fought on this moor 16th April 1746.

The graves of the gallant Highlanders who fought for Scotland & Prince Charlie are marked by the names of their clans.

Opposite, top: The windswept wastes of Culloden Moor where the last hopes of the Stuarts to the throne of Britain were forever dashed in the bloody battle of 1746. The ruthless Duke of Cumberland, whose forces outnumbered the ill-armed and ill-fed highlanders by almost two to one, gave no quarter. His opening canonnade felled hundreds and despite the immense bravery of the Scots who succeeded in breaching the English front line, they lost 1,200 of their 5,000-strong force. The casualties were so high because of an order by the Duke of Cumberland who insisted that all the wounded be put to the sword. For several days after the battle his ghoulish search parties carried out their gruesome task. Only 76 Englishmen lost their lives and to this day a series of stones mark the graves of both sides. Old Leanach farmhouse, which lies in the heart of the battlefield, still stands.

Centre: A simple engraved stone marks the scene of the carnage.

Bottom: A sword and targe, the studded shield used by the Scots to fend off attackers, have been preserved and serve as an indication of how poorly armed the Scots were.

Left: The picturesque Pass of Killiecrankie and the scene of yet another bloody battle. It came on 27 July 1689, as General McKay's troops emerged at the upper end of the pass and formed up to face James II's Jacobite troops. Viscount Dundee, who was leading the Highlanders, gave the order to charge shortly after 7 o'clock. The fierce clash lasted only a few minutes before a torrent of redcoats fled down the pass pursued by the screaming tartan terrors. Ironically Dundee was mortally wounded during the clash and died almost on the moment of victory. A stone now marks the spot where he fell. Nearby is 'Soldier's Leap' where two rocks almost bridge a deep gorge. At least one trooper escaped to safety this way.

Left: The curve of Laggan Dam, near the outflow of Loch Laggan to the River Spean, makes a powerful visual impression with its background of trees and hills. The dam, completed in 1926, is 180 feet high and 700 feet across. It provides both a reservoir, in Loch Moy, and hydro–electric power. There is a connection by tunnel with the waters of Loch Treig, farther south near Fort William.

Above: Situated on the busy A9 trunk road to Inverness the pleasant little village of Carrbridge remains comparatively unspoilt. The ancient arch of the bridge pictured here spans the Dulnain and was originally built by the Earl of Seafield in 1715 in order that funeral processions to nearby Duthil could cross the river. A more modern bridge, built in 1928 now affords tourists and winter sportsmen the same safe passage. Nearby is the modern Landmark visitor centre which gives a rare and well presented look at more than 10,000 years of Scottish history.

Queen Victoria was not amused when she cast her royal eyes over this scenery – she was bewitched, and so much so that she allowed her name to be attached to the rocky spur from which she viewed it. Admittedly the scenery has somewhat changed since Her Majesty first viewed it in 1866, due to the construction of a hydro-electric dam at the eastern end of Loch Tummel, which extended the loch by some four and a half miles, but the outlook remains breathtaking. The colourful spectacular afforded from Queen's View situated off the B8019 to the north east of Pitlochry takes in lochs, rivers, and craggy mountains. Dominating the whole scene is the snowy quartzite peak of Schiehallion. It is said that on a clear day you can see all the counties of Scotland from the chilly 3,547 feet summit but whether the astronomer Maskelyne, who conducted experiments of the specific gravity and weight of the Earth here, was aware of that is not certain. The new dam, although marring the scenery to a certain extent, includes a salmon ladder which in itself has proved a popular tourist attraction.

Right: It was in these romantic grounds surrounding Balmoral Castle, on the banks of the Dee, that some of the first pictures of Prince Charles and his then fiancée Lady Diana Spencer were taken. The seclusion and privacy afforded by its pleasant woodland setting has made Balmoral a favourite royal residence in recent years. The present residence of local white granite was built around 1853 and succeeded a former 16th-century tower of the Gordons that had been enlarged in 1830. The estate itself, which covers some 11,000 acres was bought by Prince Albert in 1852 for around £30,000 and has been used as a royal residence ever since.

Opposite, top: Nearby is the picturesque little Crathie Church which the royals attend when in residence here. Built in 1895 the church contains a royal pew and many memorials to various members of the royal family. In the churchyard near the river is the monument erected by Queen Victoria to her faithful servant John Brown. His house, across the river, can still be seen from the roadside.

Opposite, bottom: A muscular Scot gets down to the intricacies of caber tossing at the famed Braemar Games. The games, which attract contestants from all over Scotland, are normally held in September and are frequently attended by members of the royal family. Robert Louis Stevenson wrote part of *Treasure Island* in a cottage on the outskirts of the village which is now a popular tourist resort and skiing centre.

The West Coast and Islands

Previous page: Stooks stand drying in the sun at the crofting township of Torrin on the Isle of Skye. Arable farming on the island is severely curtailed by the lack of fertile ground and most crops are used to feed local livestock. In the background the impressive Black Cuillin peak of Blaven reaches more than 3,000 feet. The extraordinary looking mountain consists of a serrated hypersthene rock which in dry weather almost resembles coke.

Above: One of the first sights that will greet you when you arrive on Skye, especially if you use the popular Kyle of Lochalsh Ferry is the eerie ruin of Castle Moil at Kyleakin. Originally known as Dunakin the castle served as a fine look-out point for spotting invading Norsemen. Rumour has it that the castle was built by the daughter of a Norwegian king who strung a chain across the narrow straits to extract a toll from passing ships. Today the only tolls paid are on the ferry from the mainland.

Part of Scotland's proud geographical heritage, the west coast and islands provide some of the most spectacular coastal scenery anywhere in the world. The magnificent sights on the road to the isles – from Fort William to Mallaig – give an impressive foretaste of what is to come and leaves no visitor disappointed. It is almost impossible to suggest which season might be best to visit these shores, each has its own unique, individual charm. The calm clear views across the ocean to the Hebrides on a warm summer day are certainly pleasing to the eye, but the daunting turmoil whipped up by the savage autumn winds are no less impressive.

Skye. One of the largest and most beautiful of Scotland's offshore islands, it is only a short ferry crossing from a number of mainland ports, the most popular and most reliable being from the Kyle of Lachalsh to Kyleakin. Nicknamed, appropriately, the 'Misty Isle', Skye is a haven for those seeking solitude or good hill climbing. Although it is more than 50 mi. long, no part of Skye is more than five miles from the sea, providing varied and sometimes startling coastal scenery. A trip to the main town of Portree and the Castle at Dunvegan are well worthwhile but a favourite haunt is the tiny village of Stein on the Waternish peninsula. It offers nothing, save a post office and an inn – the oldest on the island – but the sight of a roaring peat and log fire burning in its friendly grate is a sight for sore eyes and a welcome for cold hands.

Mallaig. Though many pass through here on their way to Skye – the ferry crosses regularly to Armadale – Mallaig is an interesting tourist spot in its own right. It is a major herring port, and the surrounding scenery is among the finest of the coast. The nearby silver sands of Morar are more than a match for any in the Caribbean. Just outside the town the mysterious waters of Loch Morar, more than 1000 feet deep in places, are said to contain their own monster.

Ailean Donan Castle. One of the best restored castles in Britain, it is also one of the most photographed. Built in the 13th century, the structure stands on a tiny island where the three sea lochs of Loch Duich, Loch Long, and Loch Alsh meet. The view from the rear of the tiny cobbled courtyard is incomparable. The castle, although smashed by the Spanish and bombarded frequently by the English, has been almost completely renovated and the impressive stone-ceilinged banqueting hall restored to its former glory.

Oban. One of the main centres for the Gaelic culture and the venue for frequent highland folk concerts. It is much used by those visiting the islands of Mull, Lismore, Iona, and Staffa, where Fingal's Cave inspired Mendelssohn's overture. The bizarre but splendid structure that overlooks the bay is McCaigs Folly. Begun in the 19th century to curb local unemployment, it was meant to be a replica of the Colosseum, but it remains unfinished.

Mull. The island's main town of Tobermory is a picturesque fishing port and reputedly one of the wettest in the country. But if you can bear the weather Mull has much to offer. The narrow, single-track roads discourage a mass invasion by motorized tourists and much of the island is completely unspoilt. Salmon and trout fishing are popular pastimes and there is even a golf course.

Lewis and Harris. These islands stretch for almost 100 miles off the Scottish coast and although the beaches are as fine as those of the more exotic holiday resorts in Europe few people use them since the average summer temperature here is only 55° Fahrenheit. Surprisingly it is only a few degrees colder in winter and there is rarely a frost. Gales are recorded here more than once a week and the unspoiled beauty of the islands remains unpolluted by industry. The seafood is rich and cheap, and a visit to Stornoway, home of Harris tweed, is advisable.

North and South Uist. Spoilt by nothing save an odd rocket launcher, the miles of flat terrain here are broken up by a series of tiny lochs. The South island, made geographically more interesting by an inaccessible range of hills, sports a nine-hole golf course and trout of up to 14lb have been caught in the freshwater lochs nearby. There is an airport at Benbecula between the two islands.

Above: With its fine natural harbour Oban combines its two major industries of fishing and tourism splendidly. An excellent touring centre for the western highlands and islands it is also a centre for Gaelic culture and has a busy nightlife. Dr Johnson and Boswell found a 'tolerable inn' at Oban in 1773, today there are a wide variety of extremely comfortable hotels for the discerning tourist to choose from. McCaig's Folly, the partially completed replica of the Colosseum in Rome, was the brainchild of John Stuart McCaig, who initiated its construction in 1897 to help curb local unemployment. Offshore is the island of Kerrera where Alexander II died in 1249.

Top right: Tobermory is the principal town on the island of Mull. A busy fishing port and a sheltered bay surrounded by dense woodland makes it a popular tourist spot. It is said that an old Spanish galleon still lies beneath the waves in the bay but aside from a few coins none of the reputed treasure it contained has been recovered.

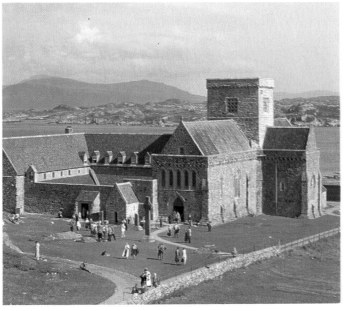

Centre: Fingal's Cave on the uninhabited Isle of Staffa can be visited by boat from Oban. The impressive 227-feet long cavern, which inspired Mendelssohn's *Hebrides Overture* is more than 60 feet high, and the depth of the water within is reckoned to be about the same.

Bottom: The impressively restored cathedral on Iona is living testimony of its religious past. St Columba is said to have come here in 563 AD to found a monastery and the island has been a centre of Christian worship ever since.

87

Right: The silver sands of Morar are aptly named and were the weather a little more reliable in summer this would undoubtedly become one of the most popular beach resorts in the world. As it is the superb sands are quiet and often deserted. A little to the east lie the deep and dark waters of Loch Morar; at around 180 fathoms it is reckoned to be the deepest inland loch in Britain.

Below: Fishing forms a vital part of Scottish industry and bustling ports like Mallaig are as functional as they are picturesque. At the end of the famed road to the isles Mallaig is a popular jumping-off point for trips to the Isle of Skye.

Far right: The column of Prince Charlie's monument overlooks Loch Shiel. It marks the spot where the Prince unfurled his standard on 19 August 1745 on his daring and romantic atttempt to recover a throne lost by the imprudence of his ancestors. The monument itself was erected in 1815 by Macdonald of Glenaladale.

The dark and sinister peaks of the Cuillins form the very backbone of Skye and although a clear view of them on this misty Isle is a rare sight indeed their presence remains dominating. The bleakest and barest of all of Britain's mountain ranges, the stark Cuillins are a maze-like irregular mass of rough gabbro on basalt and offer some of the best rock climbing in the country. Many of the steep ascents are suitable for comparatively inexperienced climbers but the ever-lurking mists that can surround the range in minutes are an ever-present danger. The most popular climb is to the summit of Sgurr-nan-Gillean which rises to 3,167 feet above Glen Sligachan. The easiest route, from the south-east, still presents many difficulties for the average climber and the presence of a guide is advisable. The most difficult, known for its adversities, is the pinnacle route and should be attempted by experienced climbers only. The highest of the Cuillins is the 3,309 feet Sgurr Alasdair. A mountaineering school lies at its foot. The fine hotel at Sligachan is a popular resting place for climbers, and lies at the crosssroads on the main road from Portree and Dunvegan to Broadford. The road from here to the north of the island affords splendid views over the rocky moors and inland lochs en route.

Far left: The tightly knit community at Portree, the capital of the Isle of Skye, is renowned for its hospitality. The tiny town, sheltered on three sides by high cliffs, makes an ideal touring centre for the island and there are a host of inexpensive hotels and boarding houses. The small working harbour overlooks the Sound of Rassay and is a veritable hive of industry. It is said that Bonnie Prince Charlie bade farewell to Flora Macdonald at a room in the Royal Hotel and Prince Charlie's cave, four miles north of the town, can be reached by boat. Ever conscious of its own heritage Portree hosts a number of spectacles throughout the year including a Highland Games and a Gaelic Mod.

Left: To the north of the capital near Loch Leathan is the high plateau of Storr. At its foot are a series of rock pillars, the highest of which is the 160 feet ' Old Man of Storr' in the centre of the picture.

Below: There are many of these traditional crofts throughout Skye and the Hebrides. Several have been converted to museums and give the visitor a rare insight into the life-style led by the original crofters of the isles.

Above left: The hostile waters of the Atlantic regularly pound the all too susceptible coasts of the Isle of Lewis yet in spite of the marine menace Stornoway with its superb natural harbour is the capital of the island's herring industry. The only town in the Outer Hebrides, Stornoway is also the main commercial, industrial and trading centre for the islands. The castle, built in 1847, is now a technical college and not open to the public but its grounds are rich with exotic plants and wildlife.

Centre left: No one has yet come to a satisfactory conclusion about the remarkable standing stones at

Callanish. Some 16 miles from Stornoway and set in the midst of bleak and barren moorland the 13-stone circle remains a mystery. An American professor who fed data into a computer deduced that they were built by ancient astronomers to predict eclipses; others believe they were laid to guide incoming spaceships from alien planets, and some believe they were the site of former Viking parliaments.

Bottom left: The sophisticated communication and travel systems enjoyed throughout most of Britain seem somewhat remote to the islanders of Barra for their incoming flights can be delayed by a freak tide. The main – and only – runway is a beach and although the adaptable tri-landers can take off and land in most conditions the most reliable form of transport to the mainland is by ship.

Above: If Stornoway and the Isle of Lewis appear remote then the neighbouring island of Harris is even more so as this isolated stretch of coast shows. Its main 'town' is Tarbert, a remote village consisting of a single terraced street that blends well with the local countryside. The Harris hotel is situated here.

Right: Situated only some five miles from the bustling Kyle of Lochalsh with its busy ferry terminal to Skye is the enchanting highland village of Plockton. Its neat little rows of immaculate white-painted cottages overlook the picturesque Loch Carron and face the Applecross and Torridon mountains to the north. A fishing village, and craft community, many original oil paintings are offered for sale in several local galleries. A homely hotel overlooks the charming harbour and offers a roaring log fire, and some excellent home-cooked food for the weary traveller. The village itself forms part of the Balmacara Estate which is now run by the National Trust. The 19th-century Duncraig Castle, in a sedate woodland setting on the lovely road towards Stromeferry, is now a school.

Above: A tiny fragment of the massive Argyll Forest Park which offers a virtually unparalleled haven for ramblers, hill walkers, mountaineers, ornothologists, and sightseers alike. Stretching for some 37,000 acres the totally unspoiled parkland is situated to the west of Arrochar and encompasses Ardgarten.

Right: The 'Five Sisters of Kintail' stamp their authority over the highland skyline on the approaches to Sheil Bridge and Loch Duich. This picture was taken from the nearby pass of Mam Ratagan now much improved since Johnson and Boswell found it 'a terrible steep to climb'. The view from the top of the largest of the sisters Scour Ouran (3,505 feet) makes the long but comparatively easy ascent well worthwhile. The tree-lined winding road that leads up Mount Ratagan and down to Glenelg is also well worthwhile.

The North

A bleak and desolate part of Scotland where one can walk 20 miles or more without seeing a single house or any sign of human habitation, the far north nevertheless offers isolationists, ornothologists, hunters and hill walkers a rare haven for their pursuits. The views from the single-track roads in the extreme northwest are remarkable and in the tiny hamlets that intermittently appear along them the visitor receives a friendly welcome. The sights here are grey, foreboding, and immense. The poet Thomas Gray once wrote, 'There are certain scenes that would awe an atheist into belief.'

John O'Groats is to Scotland what Land's End is to England. John O'Groats was originally named after a Dutchman, Jan De Groot, who set up home here in the 16th century. According to legend he argued constantly with his family over seniority and eventually built an octagonal house with an octagonal table so that no one would have precedence over anyone else. The house no longer stands, but a mound still marks the site.

Ullapool. Originally a herring port, the picturesque harbour here is much used by sea anglers and big game fishermen. There is salmon fishing in the nearby Ullapool river and an almost countless variety of other fish can be caught offshore or in the local salt and freshwater lochs. One of the more pleasant ways of viewing the local scenery is on horseback and horses are available, at a reasonable price, from the trekking centre.

Inchnadamph. This tongue twister of a fishing village lies among some of the bleakest scenery imaginable, and some of the oldest. Geologists have established that some of the rock formations in this area are of Archaean gneiss – the oldest known type

of rock in the world. Human remains thought to be more than 8000 years old have been found here and a nearby mountain has a sandstone layer that dates back 2600 million years.

Dornoch. In 1722 an old woman was burnt at the stake here in Scotland's last execution for witchcraft, but today the locals are much more friendly. A renowned 18-hole golf course and splendid fishing make this a popular tourist resort.

Wick. A busy herring port that looks directly out on to the deserted North Sea oil platforms. There is a golf course here, too, and salmon and trout can be caught on the River Wick.

Orkney. The Orkney Islands appear to have been a geographical mistake, for none except Hoy even remotely resemble the nearby mainland. Gently rolling hills and fertile green meadows make these islands more comparable to the home counties than to the Highlands. Kirkwall, the main market town, lies on the largest of the islands, Hrossey, the Viking word for Horse. Stromness, the second town, is more picturesque, with its narrow winding cobbled streets and attractive harbour.

Shetlands. Famous for more than their woollens and knitwear, the Shetland Islands are playing an increasingly important role in the offshore oil industry. The windbeaten landscapes here are virtually treeless and most of the industry was traditionally centred on the sea. The harbour in Lerwick has served as an international port for centuries and is overlooked by Fort Charlotte, built in 1665 to protect it from invaders. Hotels and restaurants are expensive but some fine fish and chip shops can be found near the harbour.

Previous page: The exact significance of the impressive Ring of Brogar, a series of massive sandstone monoliths geometrically arranged on an isolated moor on Orkney remains a mystery. Originally there were some 60 stones ranging in height from 6 to 15 feet and placed roughly 18 feet apart. The entire circle was surrounded by a trench 6 feet deep, some 29 feet wide and crossed only by two narrow banks of earth. Twenty-seven of the stones remain standing in everlasting memory of the race that put them there. One theory is that the Ring formed part of a Bronze Age temple. Another is that the stones were somehow connected with astronomy but to this day no one really knows.

Opposite: The neat whitewashed cottages of Ullapool stand out in the sunlight at the head of Loch Broom. The village set up by the Fisheries Association in 1788 makes an ideal touring centre for exploring some of the finest countryside in the North West Highlands. There are a host of excellent hotels and boarding houses.

Right: Gruinard Bay boasts one of the finest beaches on the entire west coast with its distinctive pink sands and rocky coves facing out to the Atlantic. Situated almost directly west of Ullapool in Wester Ross it can be reached by the main A832 road that leads from Braemore Junction and down past Loch Ewe and Loch Maree to Kinlochewe. The steep 1 in 6 Gruinard Hill on the approaches to the bay affords spectacular views across the island-studded waters to the Coigach Hills. The large island in the centre of the bay sadly cannot be visited as the soil is still heavily impregnated with anthrax after a series of germ warfare experiments in the Second World War. The picturesque little villages at Little Gruinard, Coast, Laide, and Ashgarve are worth visiting. Hunting and fishing are the main leisure pastimes here and there are adequate facilities for both.

Opposite, top: The craggy coastal scenery around Achmelvich Bay is typical of this part of the country. The narrow winding single-track road from Lochinver in the South leads up to Drumbeg and on to Newton and is one of the most pleasing in the north. The splendid views over the rocky and irregular coastline are breathtaking.

Centre: Scotland not only provides the best whisky in the world it also produces some of the finest glass to drink it from. Here the famous Caithness glass goblets are being fired at the glass works in Wick. Set behind Bignold Park, Harmsworth Park and the works are only a short stroll from the bustling fish market and Wick Bay.

Bottom: A popular tourist resort and market town Dornoch is also famed as the site of the last judicial execution for witchcraft in Scotland. This dated headstone marks the spot where an old woman, accused of turning her daughter into a pony which was then shod by the devil, was burnt at the stake. The magnificent golf course, said to be a match for any in Scotland, boasts magnificent views over the North Sea.

Left: The fine sands that border the Dornoch Firth make this a popular spot for bathers. The old high-roofed cathedral here was started around 1224 and despite being largely destroyed by fire in 1570 has remained a place of worship ever since. Sixteen Earls of Sutherland are said to lie in the cathedral and there is a statue of the first Duke of Sutherland done by Chantry. There is also a mutilated effigy of Sir Richard de Moravia, a brother of the founder, who was killed in the battle against the Danes at nearby Embo.

Above: Situated at the extreme north-east tip of Scotland John O' Groats overlooks the stormy and turbulent waters of the Pentland Firth. It is not, as popularly believed, the most northern point in Scotland, Dunnet Head some fifteen miles to the west is that, but the village is still some 876 miles from Land's End by road. A well stocked souvenir shop is available for the thousands of tourists who visit this isolated spot every year and rather unusual small shells, known as Groatie Buckies, can be found on the sea shore. The village is thought to have been named after a Dutchman, Jan de Groot who came to live here with his two brothers around 1500. The reason why he built his famous octagonal house is explained at the beginnning of this chapter.

Right: Only a few miles away is the impressive headland of Duncansby Head, the most eastern point in Scotland. Just off the coast lie three curious sandstone stacks best seen on a stormy winter day when the heaving seas create spectacular foaming circles around them. The sandstone cliffs of the mainland are deeply gashed in places by 'goes' and the rock has formed a natural bridge over one of the deep gullies.

Above: The interior of the
Boddam Croft House Museum
gives a rare insight into the living
and working conditions of the
old crofters. Today most live in
fairly modern houses with central
heating and proper ventilation
but a few still prefer the old ways
with the peat fire burning in the
centre of the room and the smoke
escaping through a hole in the
roof.

Top right: The spectacular sea
stacks of the coast of the
Shetlands have been formed by
centuries of weathering and
erosion. Many form ideal nesting
sites for the thousands of sea birds
that live and breed here. The
most popular in this area are
guillemots, puffins, razor bills,
shags, kittiwakes and gannets.

Centre: This remarkable three-
acre site at Jarlshof, sandwiched
between Sumburgh airport and
the sea, is one of the most
important archaeological finds in
Europe. The jumbled but still
remarkably intact remains of
three separate village settlements
lie here, the earliest of which is
said to have been inhabited by
Stone Age men around 2,000 BC.
Nearby is the Sumburgh Head
lighthouse, erected in 1820 and
designed by Robert Louis
Stevenson's grandfather.

Bottom: The busy harbour at Lerwick in the Shetlands. The solidly built stone houses in the island's capital slope steeply down to the waterfront and the hundreds of fishing vessels which come from various countries. On the last Tuesday in January locals celebrate the old-fashioned festival of Up Helly Aa when a full-sized replica of a Viking longship is burned. Overlooking the town is Fort Charlotte, built in 1665. It was intended to guard the harbour, with its mass of guns pointing seawards, but fort and the town were invaded and burned by the Dutch in 1673.

Scotland

SHETLAND

ORKNEY

Atlantic Ocean

Cape Wrath

Pentland Firth

Thurso

CAITHNESS

Lewis

SUTHERLAND

North Sea

Harris

Applecross

North Uist

ROSS & CROMARTY

Dingwall

Dornoch

Moray Firth

Banff

South Uist

Portree

Skye

Beauly

NAIRN

Inverness

Elgin

MORAY

BANFF

Rhum

Eigg

INVERNESS

Loch Ness

ABERDEEN

Aberdeen

Fort William

KINCARDINE

Stonehaven

Loch Rannoch

Blair Atholl

ANGUS

Iona

Mull

Oban

Loch Tay

PERTH

Dunkeld

Forfar

Montrose

Firth of Tay

Arbroath

St Andrews

Firth of Lorne

ARGYLL

Inveraray

DUMBARTON

Loch Lomond

Stirling

Perth

KINROSS

FIFE

Dunfermline

Firth of Forth

Colonsay

Oronsay

CLACKMANNAN

STIRLING

Glasgow

Dunbar

Islay

Rothesay

RENFREW

W LOTHIAN

Edinburgh

E LOTHIAN

MIDLOTHIAN

BERWICK

Berwick

BUTE

Arran

Firth of Clyde

Ayr

LANARK

PEEBLES

Selkirk

Kintyre

AYR

SELKIRK

Hawick

ROXBURGH

WIGTOWN

DUMFRIES

KIRKCUDBRIGHT

Dumfries

Carlisle

England

Irish Sea

Acknowledgments

British Tourist Authority 13 top & 13 bottom, 14 top & bottom, 19, 28, 29 top, 29 centre, 31, 34 top, 40, 42 top & bottom, 42 centre, 43 bottom, 52, 57, 74 centre, 74 bottom, 81 bottom, 87 top, 98, 106 bottom, 108, 111 top; Colour Library International 1, 2/3, 4/5, 6/7, 22/23, 27, 36/37, 46/47, 63 bottom, 64/65, 70/71, 76/77, 80/81, 82/83, 92, 96/97, 99, 100/101; W.F. Davidson 11, 12, 14 centre, 14/15, 16/17, 18, 20 bottom, 21, 26, 29 bottom, 42/43, 43 top, 44 top, 63 top, 72 top, 74 top, 74/75, 79, 93 top, 103, 106 top; Fotobank International Colour Library 32/33, 38/39; The City of Glasgow 30 top left & right, 30 bottom, 59 top; John Green 88 bottom, 94 centre; Michael Holford 86/87; Susan Lund 104/105; Scottish Tourist Board 48 top & bottom, 49, 59 centre, 59 bottom, 66, 94 bottom, 108/109; Bob & Sheila Thomlinson 44/45, 60/61, 68, 69, 72 bottom, 72/73, 78, 81 top, 85, 87 centre, 87

bottom, 88 top, 88/89, 90/91, 93 bottom, 94 top, 94/95, 106 centre; Judy Todd 20 top, 44 bottom, 50, 51 top & bottom, 60, 111 centre & bottom; John Walker & Sons Ltd 53 top, 53 bottom left & right; George Young Photographers 8/9, 25, 34 bottom, 34/35, 54/55, 58, 62, 110/111; ZEFA/W.F. Davidson 106/107. The photograph on page 41 reproduced by Gracious Permission of Her Majesty the Queen.

Front cover: The Pass of Glencoe: Colour Library International. Glencoe Piper: Bob and Sheila Thomlinson. Robertson tartan from p. 237 of *Scottish Clans and Tartans* by Ian Grimble, published by The Hamlyn Publishing Group Limited.

Back cover: Highland cow near Elgol, Skye: Bob and Sheila Thomlinson.

Index